SUZANNE D JOHN

Are you making these PREMARRIAGE mistakes?

lifestyles to live before and after marriage

Contents

You might possibly try doing yoga, meditation, and tea together once per week. Even if it isn't the most thrilling thing in the world on paper, a hobby that improves your mental health is always a win.

1

Marriage changes everything

The prospect of marriage is something that many women have been anticipating since they were young girls. Even though it's unquestionably a memorable and exciting experience, it's not the only significant and life-changing occasion. It's important to take your time making the descent to the altar because of this. Even if you've been dating your significant other for a decade or more, this is still true. According to life coach and author Sarah E. Stewart, M.S.W., C.P.C., marriage "changes everything." The secret, according to her, is to avoid losing oneself in the transition from being "all about me" to being "all about us." How can you be certain that you won't do that? You can begin by checking off the experiences on this list that will help you psychologically, emotionally, and physically get ready for a happy, long-lasting marriage.A new chapter in a person's life begins with marriage. There's a reason why a newlywed couple is frequently questioned about how things "feel different" now that they've said "I do." Without a doubt, the answer is "yes!" – and not just because they are married or cohabitating. When you are married, you have to learn how to compromise because you have to use the same bank accounts, you don't have as much alone time, and so on.

While some of these modifications are slight, others have the potential to significantly impact your physical and emotional well-being as well as your personality. We've identified every way your life alters after marriage, from the uplifting to the frightening.

After you get married, your spouse will be the person you spend the most time with, so you'll get to see both of their finest and worst qualities. Your vulnerability and receptivity to new experiences may increase as you become more accustomed to letting everything hang out. You'll probably feel less nervous about trying something new if you've allowed someone to get to know every aspect of you.

A 2017 University of Georgia study that looked at heterosexual couples found that following marriage, husbands grew more conscientious, which means they were more inclined to take their wives' wants into account. The difference in men "may reflect the fact that their spouses are urging them to be a little more conscientious, and reinforcing that," according to study author Justin Lavner in an interview with The Cut.

The University of Georgia study also discovered that men are likely to become more introverted over the first and a half of their marriage. In fact, it's very likely that you will both become more introverted as a couple. The University of Georgia study also discovered that marriage enhances women's emotional stability. The authors of the study hypothesize that women's neuroticism was positively affected by marriage since it subsided with time.The majority of users on the Married People of Reddit thread claimed that becoming married drastically altered the way they spend their money.

Since you can see everything your partner spends money on and vice versa, several users noted that having joint bank accounts felt weird. On the plus side, it increases your awareness of your spending significantly. Marriage, as you may probably guess, marks the end of any privacy. Your partner will suddenly be aware of all of your darkest, deepest secrets, you'll discover. Although it may seem frightening, this can actually be liberating

The way you text after getting married, especially while speaking with your husband, completely changes, as Lauren Fraser told Wedding Ideas Magazine.

"You write concise, direct texts.

A straightforward query like "What shall we do tonight?" will yield a response, "Declares Fraser

When you only wanted to know what you were getting for dinner, there wouldn't be any indication of a winky face emoji to divert you.

2

Date and Have Relationships

While not everyone has the luxury of being with other people before they say "I do," relationship experts agree that it can be tremendously beneficial in helping you know who is right for you and who is wrong for you. "When you do get hitched this will be the one thing that you are happy that you don't have to do again, but it is a process that I believe we should all go through," says Dawn Michael, Ph.D., clinical sexologist, relationship expert and author. Fran Walfish, Psy.D., a couple and family psychotherapist, agrees, adding that having relationship experience and a baseline of comparison gives you a point of reference when it comes to your future spouse.Going on dates with several people when you're young is a terrific approach to determine the kind of person you are attracted to.

However, as you age, dating ceases being an experiment in meeting new people and instead becomes a journey to meeting the one you want to spend the rest of your life with. Relationships require dating because it allows you to get to know one other better. During this time, you assess your compatibility with one another and decide whether you think the relationship has potential.One of the curveballs you could experience in your life with your partner is losing a loved one, losing your job, becoming extremely ill, or getting pregnant unexpectedly. Make sure your spouse is someone who can be patient, kind, supporting, and strong when things go tough before getting serious.

Do you and your husband know how to respectfully discuss problems in the marriage or do arguments frequently escalate into World War III? Before getting married, you should learn how to disagree politely.According to research, staying angry before bed can really have long-term detrimental effects. If you don't deal with your problems before bed, your brain starts to retain bad memories that can keep you awake and make you feel depressed.Learn the art of compromise to avoid the dangers of fights.

When it is reasonable, strike a balance and give your partner a break.

It's crucial to make an effort to understand situations from their perspective. This will enable you to identify the core problem at hand.

How well does your spouse's future vision match yours?

The fact that you get along so well and have incredible chemistry does not mean that you share the same goals in life.

The following are some crucial discussion points:

.Your address: She wants to stay in the city to be near her family, but he wants to move. **.Your profession:**He is uneasy with her giving up the financial security if she changes careers.

Your house:She wants to rent, but he wants to buy.

- **Your household :**He has never had a desire to be a parent, but she wants to be one.

  .Knowing all of these things about your potential future with someone is crucial. For instance, if it is not discussed beforehand, arguing regarding children might result in incredibly painful and resentful situations. Ask your spouse their thoughts before you get too far into the relationship to find a way out because the decision to have children must be joint. Prior to moving on with your relationship, it is essential that you both have an understanding on issues relating to money, location, careers, and families.

Before you get too far into the relationship to find a way out, ask your partner how they feel about having children. Having children must be a mutual decision. Before pursuing your relationship further, it is essential that you both have an understanding regarding issues pertaining to money, location, careers, and families. One of the most typical reasons for married couples to file for divorce is a breakdown in communication. So before you make a significant decision like moving in together or getting married, it's imperative that you and your lover learn how to communicate. Being patient while you speak and not waiting for you to pause so they may respond is a sign of a great companion.Respectful speech is another aspect of healthy communication. They don't use a disagreement as an opportunity to undermine or denigrate you. Instead, they view disagreements as chances to work out an issue.

Who a person chooses to spend time with might reveal a lot about them. Dating while in a relationship has the advantage of introducing you to your partner's close friends and family. You gain a better understanding of their social mannerisms and the kind of individuals you are choosing to associate with. Dating while in a relationship also gives you the chance to learn more about your partner's financial management skills.

Although research suggests that millennials are more willing than previous generations to talk about money, not everyone feels comfortable sharing personal financial information.

According to a Money Matters research produced by Acorns, 68% of couples indicated they preferred to discuss their weight than the amount of money they had saved. Ouch! Any mature partnership needs to have a financial discussion.

How are you going to divide your finances? Which of you has debt, and how are you going to repay it? Will you merge your bank accounts as your relationship develops or keep them separate? Is your partner financially responsible or is he or she irresponsible? Make it a point to be honest with each other about your financial situation while you're dating.Don't rush things if you're in a new relationship.

Finding your forever partner requires going on dates. Dating will enable you and your partner to become friends, improve your communication skills, and discover how your futures are compatible. Your relationship will advance toward marriage as you learn from your shared experiences.

3

Date while maintaining relationships

Live by Yourself or With Roommates

If you've been dating your S.O. since college, it might make sense to just move on in together post-graduation, but this may likely be your only chance to ever have lived separately as adults. "Living alone teaches you so many things," explains Stewart. "You learn how to be financially and emotionally independent—paying all of your bills gives you a sense of accomplishment and spending a few weekends and weekday nights alone gives you strength."To strengthen your relationship, be vulnerable with your partner (and vice versa). [1] Making your partner feel loved and ensuring they feel the same way about you are key to preserving a strong emotional bond. Tell your lover you love them and express your deepest feelings to them. You will both feel more understood and emotionally satisfied as you communicate your views and feelings more often.

[2] A healthy relationship is one in which there is equal power distribution, open communication, sharing of emotions, and mutual respect. However, your spouse shouldn't urge you to disclose every single idea or force you to be vulnerable before you're ready. It's also vital to be grateful.Develop the habit of thanking your lover every day!

Recognize their accomplishments and express gratitude when they help you.

Tell your lover what you need because they can't read your mind. Communicate openly with your partner about your concerns and your interests. Describe your emotional requirements and wants in detail. At the start of a relationship, express your needs. By being open with your partner, you are demonstrating your trust in them and expressing vulnerability. Your openness also invites them to be equally honest with you.

[3] Honesty and criticism are not the same thing. Do not criticize your partner in front of others or to them directly.
Honesty and criticism are not the same thing.

Do not criticize your partner in front of others or to them directly. Be respectful at all times and use positive language. If something is upsetting you, softly but firmly state it. For instance, you can say, "Although I adore you very much, there are occasions when a messy house makes me angry.

Can we find a solution to this?" Ask open-ended inquiries to your spouse to give them the freedom to express themselves as well. Asking questions that demand thoughtful responses will encourage meaningful communication!Feeling loved and understood by one another comes through listening to one another. Two-way communication is essential!

Give your companion your complete attention while they speak; pay close attention as you listen, and take notes on what they say. Instead of creating a response, concentrate on comprehending what they are saying.

[4] Maintain constant eye contact and refrain from interjecting during their speech.

Make a little, comforting murmur, such as "Mhmm," or say, "Go on," to show that you are paying attention. By repeating your partner's words back to them, you can demonstrate that you comprehend them. You may respond, for instance, "It sounds like work is particularly frustrating for you right now" if they discuss a disagreement at work. Determine your partner's emotional state by observing their body language. Pay attention to how they feel if they appear grouchy or exhausted, concentrate on making them feel better!

[5] Boundaries let your significant other know what you require from the relationship. Establish personal limits and guidelines for your partnership.

Get vocal assurance from your partner that they understand and will abide by each boundary or expectation before imposing them. By establishing such boundaries, you can avoid confrontation and have a talking point in case someone exceeds the line.

Boundaries may be social, financial, personal, or sexual. For instance, you could tell your partner that while you cherish your relationship and need at least one night a week to spend with friends, you still enjoy your quality time together. Each partner should refrain from attempting to control the other in a good relationship.Respecting your partner's boundaries conveys your confidence in their ability to make decisions on their own without betraying you.

Understanding your partner's expectations and limitations about intimacy, outward displays of affection, and confidentiality are examples of common boundaries.

A long-lasting, joyful, and healthy relationship depends on trust. Discuss your definition of trust with your partner. What do you believe a breach of trust to be? Does your partner's definition of trust differ from yours? Focus on developing trust once you have determined what you both require. Keep your word, support your partner when they're in need, and always be mindful of their boundaries. For instance, some people consider a breach of trust to be physical cheating but not emotional infidelity, while others consider emotional cheating to be just as harmful. Discuss your perspective with your spouse up front. Another reason you and your spouse should practice these with one another is because being open and honest are essential for establishing trust.To feel close to your lover, like going on dates and doing things together.

Even if you've been married for a long time, it's always important to arrange activities with your partner.

Decide on enjoyable activities that you and your partner will both like and designate one night per week as your designated "date night."

While it's acceptable to spend some nights at home relaxing, make sure to also do things that will take you out on the town! You can do anything you like on a date night (and romantic). You could go bowling, go karaoke, go back to a favorite restaurant, or go on a hike, for instance. Life can be hectic at times, particularly when work or children are involved. If weekly date evenings aren't currently possible, consider monthly dates instead.Your romance feels new and fresh because of spontaneity. Maintain the spark in your relationship by coming up with fun and unique ways to surprise your partner. Relationships can quickly turn routine.

Bring them on an impromptu overnight break or surprise them with a tiny gift or romantic activity. Try something that neither of you has ever done to keep you both entertained and involved.

For instance, if you and your spouse have discussed how much fun it would be to learn archery, sign up for lessons together!

When discussing your next trip, make a suggestion for a location neither of you have visited previously. Every surprise doesn't need to be a lavish expenditure. Simply preparing your partner's preferred dinner or purchasing their preferred offering them a reward after work or a passionate massage

Touch and physical affection are necessary for a strong romantic bond. Make it a point to start making physical contact to increase intimacy. This could be holding hands while walking down the street, giving them extra hugs, or giving them more kisses when the mood hits.

Discuss sex with your partner; if you two want it, take care of your sex life and be open about your wishes. Discuss your preferences, expectations, desires, and boundaries while talking about sex. It is simpler to have a fulfilling sexual life once you and your partner are aware of one another's wants. Feeling physically and emotionally close to your partner is essential to healthy relationships.Feeling physically and emotionally close to your partner is essential to healthy relationships.

There is still time to reignite that spark if you feel like you are apart.

Conflict is inevitable, and managing it politely makes your relationship stronger.

Always fight fairly; keep your attention on the issue at hand and abstain from accusing or calling others names. In order to express your feelings to your partner without making them feel attacked, use "I" statements. Then, collaborate with your partner to find a solution that will satisfy both of you.

To learn your partner's viewpoint on the situation, pose open-ended inquiries. Asking "What do you think would be the best course of action" or "How do you think this should be handled"

Instead of expressing, "You're constantly late," a "I" statement would be, "I get angry when you're late for our date night."

Keep your composure during the dispute. Take deep breaths, speak more slowly to give yourself time to think, and don't be afraid to ask for a brief break to let your temper simmer. Burying disagreements is never a good idea; even if you manage to avoid a fight, your problems remain unsolved at their root.

Instead of ignoring a disagreement, work through it with your partner.

Mutual trust is increased by sincere regrets and forgiveness. Accept responsibility for your mistakes and express your regret to your partner. Be precise, recognize your error and your partner's feelings, and then describe your plan of action for resolving the situation.

Making the initial move also makes it simpler for your spouse to follow suit and apologize if both of you have done something harmful.If your partner apologizes, it's crucial to accept their apology and forgive them as you would want to be forgiven.

As you forgive your partner, acknowledge your unpleasant emotions and then let them go. Holding onto resentments only makes a situation worse. Let them go. If your partner acted in an unforgivable way months ago, accept it and move on. Please refrain from using their prior behavior against them. Recognize your uniqueness and celebrate them. You don't have to agree on everything as long as you can communicate with one another; your differences keep your relationship vibrant and exciting.A healthy partnership will always show signs of shared development and progress. Life is full of change, and relationships also change over time. Don't let your concerns stop you from strengthening your relationship with your partner by viewing every challenge or significant change as an opportunity. During the ups and downs of your relationship, embrace change and concentrate on developing with your partner.Always keep in mind that relationship ups and downs are normal. Work as a team to solve your difficulties rather than blaming your partner for them.If relationship changes are too much for you to handle on your own, don't be hesitant to seek help jointly. You might speak with a couple's therapist or a confidante you trust.

Keeping up with other relationships helps you maintain your identity. Being in a relationship doesn't mean you're permanently glued to your partner! Balance your time spent together with time spent apart; go out with your friends, spend time with family, and engage with your personal hobbies. Encourage your partner to do the same! This way, the time you spend together is much more precious.People who value themselves equally are attracted to positivity and self-love.

When you value yourself, you're more inclined to uphold your standards and expectations and search for a mate that fulfills all of your needs. By speaking loving words over yourself, recognizing and appreciating your abilities, and engaging in activities that make you feel good, you can learn to love yourself. If you have trouble loving yourself, consider making a list of all your good qualities.

What are you good at?

What are your strongest qualities?

What would your friends say about you if they had to describe you?

4

Be financially self-sufficient

Similar to being able to live independently, being well-versed in your own money will help you feel prepared to tie the knot. Being financially independent, according to Stewart, implies you won't get married because you have to, regardless of your career or job compensation.

"You are valuable." This implies that you will be able to stand on your own two feet should you ever get divorced or separate for any other reason.

Marriage to a dependable man is acceptable. It's best if you can take care of that for yourself. When you, as a woman, consider marriage, it's crucial to consider your financial security both before and after the union. Don't just consider how to coexist peacefully with your husband or how to be a wonderful mother, should you decide to have children.Marriage to a dependable man is acceptable. It's best if you can take care of that for yourself.

When you, as a woman, consider marriage,it's crucial to consider your financial security both before and after the union. Don't just consider how to coexist peacefully with your husband or how to be a wonderful mother, should you decide to have children.

In our society, getting married mostly requires respect, strong family values, and many other outstanding female traits that have long been regarded to be crucial if a woman is to stay married.

The requirement to be financially independent, to have the mental capacity to earn and manage your own income from long before you begin to consider marriage, is not, however, discussed enough.

In a traditional sense, this might be justified by the notion that males should be expected to take care of their family in every way, negating the need for women to work and earn a living. But given that it is 2022, the days when people were ok with this kind of arrangement.

Even though males are still generally responsible for providing for their wives and children, it has become crucial for women to be as financially independent and prepared for marriage as men are in the modern marriage.

So, contrary to what we have long believed, this is not about absolving men of their obligations. Being out of touch with this concept still means being decades behind the times. It is also absurd to consider getting married before you are able to support yourself financially.

The worst situation for a woman is to be forced to remain in an unhappy marriage because she has no other financial options. And women should pursue wealth for this reason alone. Therefore, dear women, work as hard as you can since only your thoughts and your money will last forever, not anyone else. Therefore, having financial security is crucial, especially for married women. This is why.

Despite a rise in the number of working women over the previous few decades, most people still find it difficult to achieve female financial independence, especially after marriage. After getting married, women typically lose control of their finances because they either abandon their employment, combine their wealth with their partners, or just stop participating in financial decisions.Due to family pressure or usually following childbirth, women frequently give up managing their finances because it seems even mothers can't handle it. Ladies, though, giving up financial power is a bad idea. It leads to an unbalanced relationship in which the woman is frequently left at her husband's mercy without any financial independence or, worse yet, to fend for herself if the marriage disintegrates. Therefore, it is best for females to empower themselves financially, not just in terms of earning but also in terms of being financially knowledgeable and aware, as well as by participating in all household financial choices, in order to avoid such a situation.Do not immediately leave your career after getting married, especially if you are relocating to a different place. Spend some time finding a new work, exploring alternative career options, or perhaps considering self-employment there. In the beginning, especially in an arranged marriage, having financial independence is essential to maintaining the relationship's emotional and financial balance as well as giving you the assurance and conviction to leave the marriage if it isn't working out.

Even later, it will assist you in reducing your dependence on your husband for all of your requirements, essentially allowing you to handle your own bills, which is both freeing and empowering.If you continue working or launch your own business, you will have amassed enough assets and corpus to support yourself even if you divorce 10-15 years from now. Additionally, keep networking with your coworkers and other industry specialists in the event that you do need to quit your job. This is crucial if you need to pick up the pieces from the past and start looking for a career after your marriage ends. So, anticipate the best while simultaneously preparing for the worst. Don't rush to close your separate bank accounts before getting married in order to create a joint account and combine your money with the partner's.Maintain constant involvement in financial management. Because if you don't know about your husband's assets, investments, or any property that is yours or what your Streedhan is, you won't be able to claim it or have it taken into account when determining alimony in the event of a divorce.

After marriage, women frequently stop managing their finances, and if they do decide to get a divorce after 15 to 20 years of marriage, they are typically left with nothing since they have no assets, savings, or other sources of income, leaving their survival in jeopardy.

Spend some time learning about the fundamentals of finance, the assets purchased, and financial transactions, developments, and documentation.Always keep in mind that you should be the co-owner of any assets you purchase with another person, and if only your money was used to make the purchase, make sure that all of the assets are registered only in your name. Even when the wife is employed, it is typical to see the husband handle all financial decisions and investments. So, he was able to preserve the assets under his name alone.For instance, when purchasing a property, if you are a co-applicant for a mortgage, be sure you are also a co-owner. The Hindu Succession Act's Section 14 declares that a property owned by a married woman becomes her own property, regardless of whether shared money were used to buy it.Avoid signing any blank or formal paper that your husband or in-laws suggest without first reading it.

The golden guideline you should always abide by is to double-check everything before signing anything. In order to avoid paying GST or other taxes, husbands frequently launch new enterprises or make investments in their wives' names.

Women need to be aware that by doing this, they put themselves at risk. Financial responsibility may fall on you if the firm fails or encounters difficulties or if the husband is unable to make loan payments for which you have signed up as a guarantor. Therefore, don't sign a document if you don't think it's proper.Any item or property, whether mobile or immobile, that was given to you by your family or the family of your spouse during the marriage or even afterward is yours.

All assets given by the husband and his family during or after the marriage become the wife's property as part of Streedhan, while jewelry or other valuables given by the woman's parents at the time of marriage become her property as part of dowry. It is crucial that you safeguard these priceless objects and only have them in your possession.

5

Engage in a good argument with your fiance.

Conflict in interpersonal interactions is unavoidable. But it doesn't have to be upsetting or indifferent. According to experts, couples can disagree and, yes, even fight while still displaying empathy for and respect for one another.

In fact, divorce rates are higher among married couples who don't argue, according to clinical psychologist Deborah Grody. Relationships that can't be saved are those in which the spark has entirely died out or in which there was never a spark to begin with, according to her. According to Grody, when one or both couples are uncaring about their union, they don't even care enough to argue.But frequent, acrimonious, and destructive confrontation is neither healthy nor sustainable.

According to a 2012 paper released by the Society for Personality and Social Psychology, you can have disagreements with your partner in a productive way that may even bring you closer together. According to research, while expressing anger to a romantic partner can make you feel uncomfortable in the moment, doing so can also lead to open discussions that are good for the relationship in the long run.

Keep the following in mind when you and your partner are having a conflict so you can resolve it healthier and more effectivelyBe observant of your conflicts

Noam Ostrander, an associate professor of social work at DePaul University, frequently asks couples during counseling sessions, "What does the 5:30 fight look like on weekdays?"

They kind of grin because they are aware, claims Ostrander. That's because, according to Ostrander, arguments between partners frequently repeat themselves, almost like a script, without ever coming to a resolution. According to Ostrander, one partner wanting to share their day with the other but the other partner avoiding it because they both need a moment to unwind after a long day at work is a frequent reason of "the 5:30 quarrel." As a result, one partner may accuse the other of being uncaring about them, which may make the other partner feel assaulted. Instead of letting the dispute to flare up, Ostrander advises couples to identify what sets off this constant disagreement and experiment with strategies to come to an amicable agreement. Observe that you quarrel when one person gets home, and offer a novel approach to avoid that instead of sticking to the tried-and-true formula. You may suggest, "What if we simply take a moment, say or kiss hello, give it 15 minutes, and then come back together," Ostrander adds. By doing so, both partners can express their want to learn about one another's day and work together to identify the most effective approach to do so.

Conflicts are inescapable despite having even the most open lines of communication. And when they do, Grody says it's beneficial to pick a time to go through issues. If you find yourself in a heated argument, she advises saying, "Let's pick it up this evening, or another time when there will be time to discuss things."

Grody says that setting aside time to resolve conflicts gives both couples the chance to gather their thoughts and get ready. In order to overcome the inclination to be defensive or accusatory, they can consider the best method to express their emotions in a calmer, more reasoned way. In the midst of rage, things are frequently stated on the spur of the moment, according to Grody. But the words continue to haunt us.

According to Ostrander, it's typical for one or both partners to go into "fight, flight, or freeze" mode during an argument. According to him, when people believe they may be in danger, they go into one of these modes. When stress hormones become active, humans have more energy to either battle the stressor or flee the situation, which is referred to as "fight or flight." According to him, the "freeze" mode is when a person just does not react at all in the hopes that the stressor will tire of the battle.

Problem solving is extremely improbable while a couple is in this hazardous place because each individual is entirely concerned with reacting to the perceived threat they feel from their other. Additionally, Ostrander notes that if only one person is in "fight, flight, or freeze" mode while the other is attempting to mediate the conflict, it may aggravate both parties and intensify the argument.

"It can feel like they're not really listening if you're really furious with someone and they're attempting to problem-solve," he says. "I frequently suggest that someone should call a timeout in those circumstances,"Additionally, you might phrase your downtime in a way that avoids giving your spouse the impression that you are merely leaving. Maybe someone says, 'Okay, I want to talk about this. I need to calm down for around ten minutes. "I love you, and I'm not leaving," Ostrander declares. "We're going to think this through and get back to it."

Both parties will be in a better position to make significant progress when the conversation picks back up after the brief break, according to Ostrander.The same two phrases are frequently used to start fights:

"You always." People tend to jump to accusations rather than requesting their partner to do something, like tidy up around the house, according to Ostrander.

Because of the way you are asking, he responds,

"You're not getting what you want." People find it simpler to question their partners' refusal to do something than to just ask them to do it.

I'm not feeling so good, I say. The appearance of the house is causing me stress. It's more direct and considerate to ask, "Would you mind picking up some stuff?" rather than criticizing your loved one for failing to meet your needs, according to Ostrander.What makes you think that I'm not paying attention, I inquire. is lot more diplomatic than merely responding, "Well, I'm listening, so you should feel heard," to your partner's criticism, according to

Grody. When your partner is speaking, make sure to maintain eye contact and turn your body toward them to show that you are paying attention.According to Grody, these simple changes can avert innumerable future altercations.

Naturally, insults and character assassination should be avoided at all costs during a battle, according to Grody. The conversation should come to an end once there is name-calling and similar behavior, she asserts. It won't change, I'm afraid. When everyone has had a chance to cool off, couples can resume their chat.

Ostrander asserts that just as everyone has a different love language, we also have diverse apologies languages. Recognizing that you have wronged a loved one and that you must apologize is insufficient: According to Ostrander, you must be familiar with them well enough to customize your apologies to meet their needs.

According to Ostrander, "Some people want grand gestures, and some people just want to say, 'I'm truly sorry I offended you, and I will take steps not to do it again.'" Finding out what is significant to your partner is the process.

6

Explore the World

Do you recall the first time you met your partner? Consider the first time you met an ex if you're single. You didn't say you ever got bored? You didn't feel at ease either. You were always striving to impress your lover by being your best self. That makes sense. We don't want to immediately reveal our unfavorable personality qualities to a new spouse. You're probably going on a lot of dates, doing new things together, and spending actual, quality time together at this stage of a relationship, the courting phase.After spending a few years together, something unusual happens: we become accustomed to one another. It's organic. We are no longer courting our spouse because we have "won" them over. We settle into our new life together and frequently ignore both quality time and enjoyable activities. Those of you who are saying, "Crap. It's me, so don't be alarmed. All of them, that is. We must make a conscious effort to have enjoyable experiences and spend quality time with Alex while we aren't on vacation. Yes, the most of the time we are "together." We frequently work out together or attend yoga classes together, and we like to run errands together. We both work from home.It's not quality time, though. Such is life. You're merely including them in activities that you were already intending to perform. We usually have dinner together and spend the most of the evenings watching movies or binge-watching TV shows, but that isn't REAL quality time.

You may have the ideal date night every night while traveling. Focus on your partner more than your computer or mobile gadget. Remove all interruptions, and experience something new every day. NOT BE COMPLACENT, BUT PRESENT.Traveling may have tremendous highs and lows. It's a pretty enormous high to walk around the Colosseum and imagine what life must have been like during the height of the Roman Empire. A particularly irritating low is having your bikes stolen in Florence or your credit card taken in Bali. All of these things have happened to us while traveling. We experience highs and lows while traveling, which leads to our best and worst emotions. To determine if you can spend the rest of your life with someone, you must see them at their worst.You'll learn if you get along with your travel companion when you go together. Sincerity be told, you'll know very soon if you're ready for marriage and/or if this is the person you want to spend the rest of your life with.

You must work as a team to overcome the aforementioned obstacles, or you will fail. Couples learn to work as a team when they travel together. Instead, taking a trip together forces a couple to work as a unit. At home, we grow accustomed to playing specific duties. For example, Alex prepares a delicious supper, and I clean up the kitchen afterwards. She does the grocery shopping and makes sure we have the essentials at home, or I lift large objects and fix them when they break).

An individual will inevitably change during the course of their life. It is true that. Not only is growth a necessary evil, but it is also required. It would be unfortunate for someone to live their entire adult life in a static state. Can you even imagine that? Think about the person who was at his best in high school. Is there anyone who would want to marry him? NO way.

Everyone else will experience progress. Both positive and negative growth are possible. It's possible that it can be both at once. Positive personal development (career, finances, interests) frequently strains relationships. Of course, these good improvements frequently also benefit the partnership.

It is essential that a couple develops TOGETHER to prevent the concept of "falling out of love" or "growing apart" over the course of two or three decades. Couples that develop together simultaneously build both their bonds and their individual selves.We have to develop as a team because we travel together.

That is more of an observed fact than merely a conjecture. We were different people from who we are today when we first started traveling together (shortly after we started dating). Together, we have had our eyes opened, grown more enlightened and knowledgeable, overcome a variety of obstacles, and had a blast discovering our lovely globe (together).

Travel is a major part of some of our most treasured memories. Whether it was during childhood family trips or recent years of joint travel. Together, experiencing wonderful things will undoubtedly result in incredible memories that will last a lifetime. Both solo and group travel are fantastic. We've both done that a number of times. However, taking a trip as a couple is unique. One of the most amazing things you can do for a relationship before getting married is to be able to enjoy such rich experiences with the person you love. Go make some memories that will last a lifetime!

Develop the trust you both need to be successful in your marriage. Through-out your marriage, there will be occasions when your trust in one another will be tested. The key to securing the duration of the relationship is building that degree of trust when traveling together before getting married. Consider it in this way. Would you prefer your foundation (trust) to be constructed of sand so that when it is tested the entire house washes away, or would you rather it to be made of steel-reinforced concrete so that it can resist being tested, rattled, and battered by storms?Sacrificing individual lives is a catastrophic error that married and non-married partners alike make much too frequently. Yes, relationships require sacrifice and the joining of two people. However, that does not imply that people should renounce their life, friends, pastimes, etc. When you spend a lot of time traveling with one person (or maybe even just a few days for some of you), you start to irritate one other. Because you are spending every minute together, the stress of the trip is heightened. You usually only have access to a hotel room or a one-bedroom apartment, which leaves you with very little space for privacy.We will need to adjust how we operate as well as face new difficulties and rising prices. But hey, thanks to all the traveling we do together, we are experts at adapting.

Most people believe that having children after marriage follows. Many of our friends and relatives had children within a year or two of their wedding days (and some as early as literally 9 months to the day – no question whether they consummated the union). Prior to having children, it has always been our intention to be married for at least three years. Before welcoming our children into the world, we want to enjoy our new life as a married couple and lay the groundwork for their future (financially, socially, etc.).

This indicates that your window of opportunity for traveling with your spouse is just approximately 2-4 weeks before you give birth to a child, assuming you work a typical American job and only get one or two weeks of vacation. 2-4 weeks. I'm done now. That is, if you go on vacation. The majority of Americans prefer being "busy" and put in excessive hours. The most of our pals MAYBE take one week off each year.In a sense, life is fairly linear. We have this thing called the status quo, which states: You attend school until you are 18, you attend college, you graduate, you get a job you detest (if you're lucky enough to find one you detest), you find another one 1-3 years later, you get married around 30, you have children before 35, you purchase a home with a white picket fence (let's be real - our generation can't afford houses), and you raise your children and instruct them to do the same miserable things you in a sense, life is fairly linear.

You wouldn't believe it, but there are actual scientific studies that highlight the advantages that travel may offer to families as a whole, couples, and kids. It has been SCIENTIFICALLY shown that taking a trip together as a couple, and occasionally as a family, strengthens families and improves relationships. Bang. Yeah! Stupid science! Don't trust us?

Why does the honeymoon play such a significant role in a relationship? It is, in fact, extremely festive in a way that honors the brand-new union of marriage. It's (in a corny way) a tropical getaway full of sex and quality time with your partner. But shouldn't our relationships—especially our marriages—always be characterized by plenty of sex, time spent together, and warm beaches.

7

Put an end to discussing every aspect of your relationship with others.

Since there are no challenge-free relationships and problems will always arise in all relationships, expecting a challenge-free marriage would be unrealistic.There is no difficulty that couples cannot resolve together without the help of a third party because there is nothing new under the sun. Having a support system outside of your marriage is beneficial. After all, if you rely entirely on one another, you will wear each other out. But if your partner suddenly starts to confide in and rely on someone else for emotional support, don't ignore it.Sharing sensitive information about your partner's life and your relationship might lead to other types of betrayal, such as an emotional affair. Ultimately, rather than a third party, you should be the one with whom your spouse most frequently discusses their marital difficulties. Among others, a third party can be your child, your spiritual advisor, your parents, a friend or colleague, your outside interests (sports, hobbies, etc.), your in-laws, friends, or other churchgoers. The majority of these things are not inherently evil. However, they could be harmful if they get in the way of a couple's love. Working hard will be necessary to preserve your marriage.The amount it costs to maintain a marriage determines how strong it is. In other words, you appreciate the things you buy. The club of married people is closed. All other parties are excluded from the two-person contract that constitutes marriage.

For this reason, "forsaking all others" is a common term in wedding vows. The purpose of boundaries in marriage is to provide a secure environment for one's soul; outsiders can compromise this security.

To be careful with our words, we must avoid criticizing our partner in front of friends, coworkers, or clergy of the opposing sex. Why? Because doing so exposes our unfulfilled desires and wishes to people of the opposing gender at a time when our vulnerability is at its most.By making this confession in private, we are essentially inviting our husbands to fulfill our needs while also trying to feign intimacy in our marriage that isn't there.

It's possible that the other person isn't even aware that they are arousing feelings of connection or attraction in us. The problem is that once a line of exclusive, private communication is opened, Satan may easily seduce us by distorting even the most innocent gestures or by inventing inappropriate ideas and sentiments where none previously existed.

All relationships will experience disagreements at some point, but how they are handled is what counts. Here are some suggestions to keep in mind that will help you handle your next dispute in a healthy manner. How you handle a problem with your partner can influence whether your relationship is healthy or unhealthy.

1. Establish a friendly atmosphere that encourages open discussion.

You and your spouse can talk openly about what is upsetting you and what is working well in your relationship if it is healthy. In order to prevent anyone from feeling like they are doing everything wrong, it is crucial to discuss both the positive aspects of the relationship as well as the issues.A clue that your relationship can be unhealthy is if you feel that you can't communicate honestly about significant concerns, such as life issues, money, aspirations, and anything that affects or worries you on a larger scale. You may be in an abusive relationship if you are unable to express your emotions without worrying about your partner's reprisal or them being too irritated and defensive.

2. Remain cool under pressure and treat everyone with respect.

Keep your insults to a minimum toward your partner. Keep the conflict's attention on the pertinent matter; refrain from interjecting insults and slurs about the other person. Additionally, if your partner frequently becomes agitated, hostile, or begins cursing, these are indications that your relationship can be abusive. No one should yell at you, curse at you, or otherwise make you feel uneasy or afraid when you are arguing, regardless of what sparked the conflict. You shouldn't ever feel threatened or as like you need to be cautious so as not to aggravate your partner further.

3. Locate the source of the issue.

There are occasions when disagreements with your partner are the result of unmet demands. Take a time to determine whether there is a bigger problem at play if it looks like your partner is worrying over trivial things. For instance, if your partner is concerned about your ability to maintain your grades or is irritated that you are partying in the middle of the week, they may want you to set aside more time for your relationship. Think about the situation from your partner's perspective and consider how you would feel if the positions were reversed. Instead of merely attempting to get your message over, be considerate of your partner.

4. Be wary of arguments that are motivated by a desire for control.

It is a HUGE red flag if you suspect that your partner is attempting to restrict what you do. If your spouse gets upset when you text other people, doesn't like it when you put work and obligations before them, pressures you to hook up with them, or attempts to limit your time with friends, these are all indications that they might be trying to exert control over you. No one should ever try to control you, especially not your spouse, even if they try to justify it by stating they "I'm just over-protective," "it's my trust issues," or it's "because I love you."

5. Try to find a middle ground.

It's crucial to strike a balance between what each partner wants and feels comfortable doing. You will reach an understanding on issues without feeling as like you are making significant compromises for your relationship if you both want to make it work. Conflict resolution often involves making compromises, and it might be simpler than you think to reach a middle ground! Alternate days to spend time with each friend group, or spend a night alone, if you and your partner are fighting over seeing your friends or your spouse's friends. Ask your partner to contribute the next time you go grocery shopping if you feel like they are constantly devouring all of your food.

6. Choose your battles wisely and agree to disagree.

Sometimes it's important to question whether the issue at hand is indeed worth fighting over. Is the only decision to be made what to eat for dinner? Using the same covers? What should be your upcoming Netflix binge? Sometimes it's best to just ignore a little issue. It probably isn't worth your energy if you won't still be upset about it the following week. You won't always agree with your partner, so if you believe the disagreement is too significant to ignore, you should ask yourself whether you two are truly compatible.

7. Think about whether or not the problem is solvable.

Sometimes we fight with our partners over REALLY important issues that affect our lives, such as whether to change schools, whether to have children, and where to reside after graduation. Consider whether the relationship is truly worthwhile if you believe that you will have to compromise your ideals, principles, or aspirations in order for it to function. For a relationship to succeed, you and your partner should see eye-to-eye on the bigger picture.

One of the key components of compatibility is sharing similar values, views, and dreams with the other person.

You'll be able to resolve arguments in the future in a healthy and beneficial manner if you keep these suggestions in mind when you're having your next argument. Even if it means you get to turn into birds together in the end, nobody wants to be like Noah and Allie from The Notebook, who never agree on anything and fight all the time. Constant bickering, heated arguments, and conflicts that get out of hand are all indications of a troubled marriage.

Develop a Hobby or Two

Hobbies give you your own time and space, which will be helpful when you start a marriage, according to Stewart. They also make you more interesting.

Having a way to express yourself and reduce tension and stress in your life, whether it be through running, reading, writing, yoga, or meditation, can make you a better spouse and a happier person in general.Finding shared interests and pastimes can reduce marital tension and reinforce the notion that you and your partner work well together.

He enjoys doing "boy activities" like playing sports, collecting baseball cards, or going hunting. This is a prevalent topic among married couples. She enjoys "girly" activities like sewing, scrapbooking, and writing about deals. She enjoys any movie that has the line "based on the novel by Jane Austen" in the credits, whereas he prefers Saving Private Ryan. He could eat steak and potatoes for every meal, while she likes to try all types of cuisine from around the world. And so forth.Certain aspects of these activities undoubtedly highlight the inherent distinctions between men and women. Given their distinctive personalities, skills, and experiences, it is quite acceptable for husbands and wives to have diverse likes and dislikes. Couples using the assumption that "his interests" and "her interests" should take precedence over one another at all times would be making a big error.The chance to interact with one another is lost when husbands and wives are too preoccupied with "doing their own thing." Finding shared interests and pastimes can reduce marital tension and reinforce the notion that you and your partner work well together.The chance to interact with one another is lost when husbands and wives are too preoccupied with "doing their own thing."

When was the last time you considered your spouse to be a friend—someone you love being around and who you can engage in activities with that will pleasure both of you? Husbands and wives are missing out on a crucial aspect of marriage if they are adept at their duties as lovers, parents, and partners but are unable to comprehend what it means to be friends. Solomon's description of romantic love in the Bible: "This is my lover, this is my buddy" puts the idea of friendship front and center (Song of Songs 5:16b, emphasis added).You could occasionally feel bored when you transition into rest mode from your busy and repetitive job life. But it's also up to you to make this downtime more worthwhile by doing something with it!

There are hobbies accessible nowadays for every age and preference. You can add a new challenge to your life by picking what you think you can do from this list of hobbies. You probably think of shared interests when you consider hobbies. However, pursuing various and unusual activities makes having a pastime more fun and fulfilling.

In most cases, finding a pastime as an adult involves one of two outcomes: either you've had an interest for your entire life and have remained with it, or you can't seem to find one at all. Even yet, finding time for hobbies can be challenging when you have a busy schedule with family, job, and life in general.

Choosing enjoyable pastimes for couples? That might be considerably trickier. You must not only find the time to engage in a hobby you can return to week after week and month after month, but you must also choose a hobby that you both genuinely love doing together. A fantastic example of a hobby that you and your spouse might enjoy independently but not necessarily together is reading. Perhaps your tastes in books are different or you read at different rates.

This is why it can be beneficial to discover an activity that both of you are utterly unfamiliar with. So, if there is a learning curve, both of you will experience it and can progress together rather than feeling behind at any one time. Coltrane Lord, a specialist in conscious partnerships, says that engaging in enjoyable activities with a partner should push each person to grow and enable the development of a more profound and expanded connection. "Participating in new hobbies and learning something new together are fantastic methods to kindle greater passion and strengthen bonds,"

Here are 11 enjoyable pastimes you may enjoy with your sweetheart.

1.Volunteering

Together, volunteering can have an influence for a variety of reasons. First of all, it may compel you and your spouse to talk about the causes that are most significant to you. Second, sharing an experience together can help the two of you become closer. The third and most significant benefit is that it can help those in need in your community. It need not be monotonous either. You can walk dogs at a nearby shelter if you two share a passion of animals. If you two share a love of the arts, you might volunteer to give local youngsters free art lessons.

Lord says that helping a cause that appeals to both of you while volunteering is soul-satisfying. "You will both share a sense of service that not only benefits others but also gives you both the chance to experience gratitude and compassion."

2. Physical exercise

Even if you both enjoy working out, you probably don't work out together every day. Perhaps you enjoy spinning or weightlifting while your companion enjoys running. It would be a terrific idea in this situation to turn this passion of physical activity into a new, shared pastime. Think about doing something new for both of you, like golf, surfing, hiking, tennis, bicycling, or any other sport.

According to Lord, exercise increases endorphin production and increases the likelihood that you will release tension from that activity rather than from other activities.

3. Anything creative

Finding time to be artistic might be challenging for those of us who aren't professional artists but yet like painting, drawing, or doodling in our spare time. Most people don't have time for arts and crafts in their hectic daily schedules, but if you enjoy the same hobbies as your partner, it will be simpler to find time for them. You might be surprised to learn how much better for your relationship the experience can be.

Painting, sculpture, photography, picking up a musical instrument, or sharing a poem are all sexy activities that give variety to your life, according to Lord. You two can serve as one other's creative inspiration and compare the results.

4.Meditation

The concept of meditating with your partner usually elicits one of two responses from you: "Well, that seems like a peaceful activity!" also, "How on earth is that meant to be fun?" However, Lord asserts that the technique may have a greater effect than you might imagine. In addition to reducing tension and fostering inner serenity, Lord claims that this exercise will also strengthen your spiritual bonds.

You might possibly try doing yoga, meditation, and tea together once per week. Even if it isn't the most thrilling thing in the world on paper, a hobby that improves your mental health is always a win.

5.Travel (Even Just In Your Own Neighborhood!)

Traveling right now looks a lot different than it did, but prioritizing discovery and new adventures in your relationship doesn't have to change. Odds are there are still parts of your city, town, or state that you can explore if you make a point to do it.

"Traveling to new places and experiences new things is a great way to add dimension and texture to your life and relationship," Lord says. "The challenges help you grow, while the diversity helps you to evolve as a couple.

Try making a point to visit a new neighborhood in your city every month, or driving on a mini road trip to a local tourist attraction every once in a while. You'll learn more about your community and, more importantly, each other.

6.Cooking

Regardless of who in your partnership is a better cook, mastering a new cooking technique together can be both difficult and gratifying. Perhaps you two can learn to bake together, or you can each concentrate on a certain cuisine that you are unfamiliar with. Maybe you may learn more about wine or enroll in classes taught by professionals.

Lord emphasizes the idea that cooking and eating together can be such a satisfying and sociable activity by saying, "Cuisine feels like home, and you get to nurture each other's bodies with delicious and aromatic food."

Another thought? Nicole Moore, a famous relationship guru, advises making it a challenge. Create a weekly activity where you and your partner compete in a cook-off, advises Moore. "Choose a recipe, and prepare the same dish with your spouse. The biggest dessert bite goes to the winner!

7.Dance

Dance is a great hobby for couples since it mixes creativity, exercise, intimacy, and fun. It can get you moving, physically bind you to one another, and be a wonderful way to enjoy a different kind of music or culture. Make dancing a habit, advises Lord. "Movement, imagination, music, and laughter are always effective treatments."Lord's recommendation is echoed by Moore, who points out that taking dancing lessons online may be done without ever leaving your home. Moore advises finding a beginner's Salsa or swing dancing class on YouTube and having fun with your partner by acting silly'

8.Crosswords

It's vital to have a shared activity that you can engage in at any time, anywhere, and in whatever phase of your relationship or your life. Crosswords might seem dull, but you can play them with your spouse for the rest of your lives—on airplanes, in cars, before bed, over supper, in waiting rooms, etc. Both of you may find it stimulating to use your brains in novel and difficult ways.

It can become a treasured custom and hobby for the two of you that you can carry into any stage of your lives if you decide to do a crossword together once a week while having dinner or while sipping on your favorite drink. That's quite amazing.

9.Fishing

According to matchmaker Bonnie Winston, it might be time to give fishing as a hobby another thought if you haven't already. Couples can easily share this activity, and it's a wonderful way to strengthen their relationship. Romance will undoubtedly be sparked by the crisp air, the deep blue sky, and the rural setting. The fishing equipment can be purchased or rented, says Winston, who was inspired by the fly-fishing film A River Runs Through It. "Cook that trout meal together and enjoy it in your hut in the woods by the fire after the fishing trip." Doesn't that seem shockingly sappy?

10. Gardening

Whether you have a large outside area or a little patio, gardening is a terrific way to strengthen your relationship with your significant other and enjoy the fruits (or vegetables) of your labor for several weeks. You can plant some herbs on a windowsill or go all-out for spring and do a complete raised garden bed in the backyard, filling it with tomato plants and other delicacies.

Anyone who has ever tried picking weeds is certainly aware of how terrific of a workout it can be, but it may also be an opportunity for you both to learn something new. Additionally, because plants need routine maintenance, neither of you will be able to ignore the pastime.

11.Taking a Language Course

Together, you and your spouse can go through the extraordinary experience of learning a new language from scratch. What else can you both claim to have learned together, from scratch? You could even set a challenge for yourself, like promising to learn French in two years and to celebrate with a week at a lovely chateau in France.